Preface

This book was designed to enhance the experience of those who have celebrated the "Many Faces of Old Glory" at a live performance or by video. We hope this book will bring back many exciting moments from Vane Scott's presentation.

For those who have not experienced the "Many Faces of Old Glory" this book, when read in conjunction with the enclosed CD, will supply the listener with a visual/audio experience that is as close to attending the concert as possible.

On it's own, this book is an exciting experience in understanding how we got our American Flag and a historical treasure of the people and places that made us "One nation under God."

Ed Watson
publisher

A SPECIAL THANK YOU

We express our thanks to the National Flag Foundation (NFF) for permission to copy flag scenes from their impressive collection of original paintings considered to be the largest set of matched U.S. Flag art in the country. NFF commissioned 40 historical flag scenes, of which 14 are used in the book.

In all, NFF commissioned 48 paintings by two artists, Don Hewitt and Calvin Lynch. The originals are housed in the Flag Room at Flag Plaza the home of National Flag Foundation in Pittsburgh, Pennsylvania. Copies are available on the poster, Flags of America available from National Flag Foundation.

NFF is a private, nonprofit corporation with roots dating back to 1898. They are known as America's Flag Authority, and The Voice of Flag Education. Their mission is to develop multi-media educational resources for the pre K-12 schools that provide instruction in respect for the Flag, pride in our country, and responsible citizenship. Their Young Patriots Educational Series is in schools around the nation.

Vane Scott, author of this book, and National Flag Foundation have worked together for many years to promote flag education. We urge you to look at the NFF Web site www.AmericanFlags. org for more information, or e-mail at flag@AmericanFlags. org.

VANE SCOTT'S
MANY FACES
OF
OLD GLORY.

Vane Scott's "Many Faces of Old Glory"

Published by:

Witness Productions
Box 34, Church St.
Marshall, IN 47859
765-597-2487

ISBN 1-891390-20-1

Student Edition
ISBN 1-891390-23-6

Front Cover: Vane Scott with the Grand Union Flag under which we fought
the early battles of the Revolutionary War.

Back Cover: The drawings off Don Hewitt and John B Rodgers.

5 Star cut for the Betsy Ross Flag © 1995-2006 by the Independence Hall Association

Printed at Walsworth Publishing, Marceline, MO.

www.vanescott.com

Acknowledgements

Dr. Whitney Smith, PhD, Director
Flag Research Center-Winchester, MA

National Flag Foundation, Pittsburgh, PA Flag Art

Independence Hall Association

John B. Rodgers, Brazil, IN additional Flag Art

Tuscarawas Philharmonic, Dover, Ohio
Eric Benjamin, Composer & Conductor

Publisher, Ed Watson

Dedicated to

My parents who introduced me to show business and performing, and my maternal grandmother who always told me I would be the one in the family to make it in show business.

And, to my wonderful wife Barbara, who has helped me stay on track, to arrive where I am today. Without her 55 years of enduring love, companionship and partnership, I would probably be sleeping under a bridge.

And, to all the dedicated teachers that will be using this book to educate their students on why it is so important that America survives and that the future of their country will someday be in their hands.

"The best of America must endure....it simply must."

Vane Scott

Nationally renowned for his live performance of Many Faces of Old Glory and his video Many Faces of Old Glory: The Concert, Newcomerstown resident Vane Scott has been presenting the show for 30 years. His video has been recognized as the best selling, privately produced video in America and Vane Scott is still performing the show "live" all across the country. The presentation is considered by many to be the finest ever produced on how we got the flag and how we got the United States, and has been deemed by educators all across America as suitable for all ages.

Vane Scott has earned the credibility to tell the story of the flag, having served in the Navy, in the South Pacific during World War II, aboard the destroyer USS Radford, DD 446, one of America's most decorated destroyers. After the war he was a professional supper club entertainer and a big band vocalist, and later was in the decorating and parade float business, as "Great Scott" Displays for 20 years, decorating entire cities for fairs and celebrations. He helped decorate Washington D.C. for President Eisenhower's first inaugural, was official Decorator, Floatmaster, and driver for two Miss Americas, and designed and built most of the floats for the Pro Football Hall of Fame, while decorating the entire city, until 1969. He has been a writer, a commercial artist, and has appeared many times on radio and television. He performed over 2,000 live shows coast to coast, including Branson & Pigeon Forge for Veteran's Week, as well as many national and state conventions, and has been on the same show bill with some of America's biggest stars before audiences as large as 20,000.

In 1968 he and wife Barbara started the Colonial Flag Company and after 25 years retired from that. Colonial now operates the largest U.S. Flag lines in the world.

Along with his recent induction into the Ohio Veterans Hall of Fame, Vane has received the prestigious State of Ohio America Legion "Red, White & Blue" Award and has also received awards from the VFW and the "Patrick Henry Award" from the Military Order of the World Wars. He was presented the "Spirit of Freedom" award for a lifetime dedicated to promoting patriotism.

Vane Scott resides in Newcomerstown, Ohio with Barbara, his wife of 53 years. They have three grown children, four grandchildren and five great grandchildren.

Foreword

Throughout our great country we see groups and individuals who are fighting to preserve the patriotic values that surface in time of national crisis and days of celebration. In the days that followed the numbing events of 9/11, a record number of American flags were flown across the country. At one point during that time, anyone who had worked in the Flag manufacturing industry was called to come back. One grandmother-type seamstress was asked why she was working and not home making cookies. To paraphrase her reply: my country called and here I am.

One of our Navy Veterans, a tireless patriot and freedom fighter, is Vane Scott, author of this book. He owned and then sold the flag factory in which the seamstress grandmother worked. We at National Flag Foundation have been associated with Vane for many years. Loving his country, his earnest desire is to pass the heritage of freedom and liberty, as embodied in the American Flag, to students and Americans in general. He has worked for many years researching facts, writing music, making corrections, and performing for live audiences as the voice for the U.S. Flag. He has inspired millions with his performances and videos. And now we have this important book to enhance and preserve patriotism and respect for our Flag. This Book and the accompanying CD are not just for entertainment. They are for parents and others to teach their children and for teachers to use in the classroom. You will learn about origins of the U.S. Flag, American history, and values of citizenship. The Book is a welcome addition to Vane's contributions to patriotism in America.

Clark D. Rogers
Director of Educational Programs
National Flag Foundation

READER: AUDIO BOOK BEGINS HERE.

INTRODUCTION

Every American should know
the story of America.
Each generation must be
reminded that freedom
is not free.

The men and women of today
are obligated to pass on to
future generations
the great gift of freedom
for which our forefathers
gambled their all.

Vane Scott

THE 69TH SEASON

TUSCARAWAS PHILHARMONIC

ERIC BENJAMIN, MUSIC DIRECTOR & CONDUCTOR

MANY FACES OF
OLD GLORY, II

VANE SCOTT

SATURDAY • MAY 21 • 7:30 pm

"I am an American!"

Have you ever looked into the eyes of an immigrant that has just become a new United States Citizen?

One who took the long and difficult journey from poverty and hopelessness, pledged their loyalty, and allegiance to our flag and now are ready to start a new life.

You can see the hope, the dreams, the eagerness that lies within.

Now, they can have a real life, one that means a future for their children that was never there for them.

Now they too can proudly say,

"I am an American!"

We hope, after you have seen this show, and you leave this place, you will tell your children and grandchildren and great grandchildren how important it is for them to understand why we love this country so much.

After all, they are the future of America and they must have that same eagerness to join in the American Dream......
or, through ignorance and their own prosperity, they could lose it all.

The United Kingdom Flag

Before I tell you the story of how we got our flag and how we got the United States, I'm gonna tell you a story about how another country got their flag, one you'll be familiar with.

The oldest flag that's still being used today began way back in the year 1200 when the English knights were coming back home from the Crusades. They were passing through the city of Genoa, Italy, and they saw a piece of cloth waiving on poles all over the city, and they liked what they saw. It was called a flag...

John B. Rodgers

The flag is called the "St. George Cross." Just a simple red cross on a white flag.

Now there are a lot of other countries in the world that still use this design. Like Norway, Sweden, Denmark Finland, only in different color combinations.

The "St. George Cross".

Now the English took this home with them and adopted it as the official flag of England.

Four hundred years later there's a queen on the throne of England, Queen Elizabeth I. This is still her flag but she's fighting a different war now. She's fighting Scotland, one of the worst wars in history.

Her troops are under the "Cross of St. George".

The Scots are fighting for a king, King James of Scotland. And he has a cross.

Only his is a little different. His is called the "Cross of St. Andrew".

Now this is still a popular flag today, so if you see somebody running around and flying this in their front yard, you'll know they're pretty proud to be of Scottish ancestry.

John B. Rodgers

So here we have the two armies fighting this terrible war under the two crosses.

Queen Elizabeth I is so busy being one of the best Queens England ever had, she never had time for romance.

She could never find the right guy.

Now, if you've kept up with English Royalty in recent years, that part hasn't changed a bit, has it? Ha! Ha!

Well, unfortunately Queen Elizabeth I died in 1603 and left no heirs to the throne of England.

She's the last of the royal blood.

Where are they going to find a relative to sit on the throne?

There's none left in England.

They're looking all around and they found a distant cousin.

Who was it?

The man they're at war with....King James of Scotland!

But he's the enemy!

Well, they have to ask him anyway.

"Will you be our King?"

He's thinking, "If I'm King over both sides that'll end the war!"

So, in 1603 he ascended the throne of England as James I.

But the fighting didn't stop because now they're going to fight over which flag to fly.

The English want to keep the "Cross of St. George".

It's been their flag for four-hundred years.

But the Scots, they're saying, "Well we want our flag cause that's our King on the throne."

Before this gets into another war James better do something in a hurry.

He figured out how to make everybody happy.

You see, all he did was put both crosses on one flag.

Now this is called "The King's Colors" in your history books.

It came to North America to the first permanent settlement here we named after this king, Jamestown.

It came back again on the Mayflower in 1620.

"The King's Colors".

Don Hewitt

THE KING'S COLORS

Don Hewitt

About 100 years later there's another Queen on the throne, Queen Ann.

She doesn't want to fly the King's colors, she's the Queen.

So, she redesigned the flag of England and she stuck those "King's Colors" up in the corner of her "Red Ensign".

John B. Rodgers

This is called the "Queen Ann" or "British Red Ensign".

Some of the more adventuresome folks called it the "Red Meteor".

This is the flag England flew when she colonized the world.

It came to North America.

George Washington will fight against this flag in our revolution, and it will play a very important role in the development of the flag of the United States.

So remember it.

I'm going to show it to you again later.

The "Queen Ann" or the "British Red Ensign".

About 100 years later England took in Ireland and became the United Kingdom; England, Scotland, Ireland. (Note: This event is several years after the British surrendered the colonies).

Ireland has a skinny red cross they call the "Cross of St. Patrick".

Somebody said, "Let's put that on the same flag with the other two crosses.

So, in 1801 the flag of the United Kingdom was born.

All three crosses.

See that skinny red cross, that's Ireland,

the "Cross of St. Patrick".

John B. Rodgers

John B. Rodgers

Now this is still the flag of the United Kingdom today and it's known around the world as the "British Union Jack".

What about our flag?

There are many versions of how we got the flag of the United States.*
I call mine the "Many Faces of Old Glory" and you'll sure know why when we get
to the end. These people your going to hear about, and the incredible things they did
is all based on truth.
They not only gave us our flag, They gave us our country, because you can't tell the
story of how we got our flag without telling how we got the United States.

John B. Rodgers

Now this isn't a history lecture tonight. There's some humor in some of these
stories. Boy, I hope your going to laugh when it's funny. Ha! Ha!
Your going to thrill when it's thrilling
and there are some sad places too.

* **I research my stories from several sources to get the best and most accurate picture of the actual events.**

And now the story.....

"A moth-eaten rag
on a worm-eaten pole
does not seem likely
to stir a man's soul.
'Tis the deeds
that were done
'neath the moth-eaten rag
when the pole was a staff
and rag was a flag."

Don Hewitt

The year is 1770, we have 13 colonies on the east coast. We're occupied by King George's army. We're not allowed to own our own ships. We can't have military weapons or trained military units.

Well, the King figures out, it's costing him a fortune to keep his army of occupation here. So, a few years earlier than this he had what was called the Stamp Act passed in Parliament over in England where we had no vote.

A heavy tax on the colonies.
Boy, did we get mad about that!

"Taxation without representation is tyranny!", we said.

The colonists were so mad they rioted against the troops in Boston.
It became known as the Boston Massacre.
There's a monument down in the old square in Boston
that has the names of those first Americans that
died for the cause of freedom.

And we can't recite any of their names.
But we ought to know the name of the first guy
on the list.   His was Crispus Attucks......A black man!

John B. Rodgers

Now, the year is 1775. We're still under the thumb of the King.
We're under guard by the army.

But the world finds out about us.
They're sending ships.
We're trading, making lots of money.
But, the heavy tax on the colony's tea is really boiling now.
There's again the calls of,
"Taxation without representation is tyranny!"

 We want to vote on our own tax money. Spend it here on roads, and bridges
and schools, maybe new voting machines in Florida. Ha! Ha!

Well the king still ignored us, so we got madder.
Now we're forming secret societies and clubs and organizations. We're stealing
guns and ammunition. There's talk of a rebellion against the King.

Somebody said, "We're secretly training an army in the woods!"

Now these groups are starting to get names. The Minutemen, the Militia, the Sons of Liberty, the Oak Ridge Boys!....... Ha! Ha!

I just wanted to see if you were paying attention. Ha! Ha!

(One night I called them the "Sons of the Pioneers.")*

Now, it's April 18th, 1775, and a Boston silversmith learns that the British troops, under General Gage, are going to march from Charlestown in Boston to Lexington.

They're going to arrest two of our greatest patriots for treason. Then they're going on to Concord to confiscate the guns and ammunition they found out we've got hidden there.

They're going to squash the rebellion.

Well, Paul Revere is about to ride into history.
He and his friend, Mr. Dawes mount up.
Paul Revere stopped at the Old North Church when he found out the direction and route the troops were going to take and he had a signal lantern hung way up in the belfry so the other riders would know, and they began the ride.

John B. Rodgers

They're pounding on every farm house and village and hamlet door along the way,
"The Regulars are marching!
The British are coming!"

When they got to Lexington, seventeen miles away, they pounded on the door of Capt. John Parker.

He's the head of the local Minutemen.

*King of the Cowboys, Roy Rogers' singing group.

They say something like, "John, John, they're coming to arrest Samuel Adams and John Hancock for treason. They're going to take our guns!"

And they rode off into the night.

Well, Captain Parker knew what to do. His men are mad, they're ready to fight. He sounded the alarm. And a hundred and seventy men answered the call. They're running out of farms and villages and little towns carrying squirrel guns and pitch forks and clubs and the craziest looking flag you ever saw. They gathered on the green near the bridge.

Boy we're waiving that flag. We're going to fight the army!

Well we looked across the bridge.

There wasn't anybody there. We got there too quick. The army was hours away and Capt. Parker saw his men cooling down. He says, "You know, you guys might as well go on home. They're not going to be here for awhile.

I'll call you back when they get closer."

Well, everybody went home.
Now they've got a chance to think about this dumb thing they're doing.
Can you imagine? Going against the King's army with a squirrel gun.

These guys aren't soldiers.
They're farmers, and merchants and hunters,

and they're going to fight a war,
not in a foreign land.
This is going to be right in they're own front yard!

Pretty soon it's after midnight.
Nobody could sleep, you know.

These guys are tossing and turning.
Every fast horse in the night they hold they're breath to see if that's going to be the alarm.
Finally at 4:30 a.m. on April 19th, 1775. Captain Parker sounded the alarm again. They went back to the green. The guy with the flag is back. Boy we're ready to fight again.

Well......this time they were there!

The commander looked across the bridge and saw all these mean-looking guys with the squirrel guns and pitchforks.

He says, "Lay down those arms and step aside!"
Captain Parker said, "No! Stand your ground.
Fire only if fired upon, but if they want to have a war let it begin here!"
Well that didn't scare the commander.
He said, "Lay down those guns in the name of the King!"

Captain Parker looked at his men the second time
 Now, they're trembling with fear, ill-equipped, ill-trained.

And he looked across the bridge at the best equipped,
best trained army in the world.

What's he going to do?
Well, he'd better get them out of there.!
"Retreat!
Take your guns with you.
We're going to fight another day!"
Everybody is running around trying to get out of the way! BANG!

"By the rude bridge that arched the flood,
they're flag to April's breeze unfurled.
Here once the embattled farmer stood
and fired the shot heard 'round the world."

Ralph Waldo Emerson

The revolution has begun!

The flag they carried that day is called the BEDFORD FLAG, because the man that carried it that day ran all the way from the little town of Bedford, down the road, to get in the fight.

His name was Nathaniel Paige.

They've traced this flag back through his family almost one hundred years before. It's still there today, in the museum, considered to be one of the oldest flags in North America.

The Latin on this flag means, "Conquer or die.".......

Some of us died that day!

THE BEDFORD FLAG

Don Hewitt

But we beat them!

We beat the King's army there, because we didn't fight like they did.

Back in the old days, the big armies of the world......

Boy were those guys dumb. They'd stand in close tight ranks and shoot point blank at each other, like ducks in a shooting gallery.

They were crazy.

We couldn't fight that way.

We didn't have enough guns.

I hope we were smarter than that.

We fought Indian style.

We hid behind walls and in the ditches, behind the trees and in the houses.

We picked them off all the way back to Boston.

They're losses were terrible.

Many years later, a letter was found that was written home by one of those British officers that was in that terrible march. He wrote it the following day while it was all still fresh in his mind. And in his letter he paid a tribute to our Colonial Minuteman when he wrote...

> "Whoever looks upon them as an irregular mob will find himself very much mistaken. Nor are they void of a spirit of enthusiasm as we experienced yesterday. For many of them concealed themselves in houses and advanced to within ten yards to fire at me and other officers, though they were morally certain of being put to death themselves, in an instant!"

John B. Rodgers

Well........we beat the King once.
 If we had a leader, could we beat em again?

Who'll we get for a leader?

Well the best known military man of the time was
George Washington. So, we asked him. "Will you lead
our army against the King?   We want to vote."

John B. Rodgers

Well, Washington is for the cause, but he knows there's no army out there.
There's a bunch of guys running around out in the woods with squirrel guns and
pitch forks. But, he says, "You know, I've made my fortune in America. I'll put
up my own money to outfit and train the first thousand men. When they're ready
to fight, I'll take command and we'll show the King."

That's what we did!

But, where's he going to get all these cannons and guns it takes to fight a
revolution?
 Nobody could get in to help us.

The British have the biggest navy in the world.
The whole east coast is blockaded.
But, Washington found out a secret.
The King's army had a lot of cannons and guns stored down in the Bahama
Islands, in the caves, off the east coast.
They knew we couldn't go there.
We're not allowed to own ships.

So.....Washington is thinking, "You know, if we could borrow a ship from Carnival Cruise Lines......... Ha! Ha!

Well he can't do that.

I thought, why doesn't he wait a couple years, till they build the White House. Then he can run it like a Holiday Inn and get all the money he wants to build the ships. Ha! Ha!

Well you know he can't do that.
Then he remembered something
really important......
he had married one of the richest
women in North America!

John B. Rodgers

I saw her picture.
Boy she must have had a lot of money ....
I'm sorry Martha. Ha! Ha!

So he asked her, "Will you help me?
I've got to have enough money to build six ships secretly."

Well you know she's going to help her husband.

Evidentially she did. She gave him her "Visa Card!" Ha!
Got the ships built. Now he's got to find sailors to sail the ships.
And he found them.

Now he's got to have a landing party. Somebody's got to go ashore when they get there and do the dirty work.

And he found them.

Now they're ready to go.

They secretly set sail down the inland waterway and all six ships are flying the PINE TREE FLAG.

THE PINE TREE FLAG

Don Hewitt

Well that's a good name for this flag but they called the ships Washington's Cruisers.

I think I'd have called them Martha's Cruisers.

Wouldn't you?

I mean, she paid for them.

The landing party, Colonel Chistopher Gadsden's men. Well, he wants his flag flying from the six ships too.

The GADSDEN FLAG looked like this!

Well this always get the attention of the boys in the back row, I'll tell you.

Ha! Ha!

Everybody got there safely. These guys went ashore, did in the British guards, took all the cannons and guns and brought them back to start the rebellion.

Who were these guys?

Colonel Christopher Gadsden's men?

Well, if you follow them up through history a couple more years, they became the United States Marines!

So, the next time you hear "From the Halls of Montezuma to the shores of Tripoli", remember, it started on the beaches of the Bahamas under a Rattlesnake flag.

DONT TREAD ON ME

THE GADSDEN FLAG

Don Hewitt

Now, it's 1776, Washington is ready. He mounts up and joins the Philadelphia Light Horse Troop.

They're going to escort him to Cambridge Massachusetts where he is going to take command of the Continental Army of the Colonies!

PHILADELPHIA LIGHT HORSE TROOP FLAG

Don Hewitt

The PHILADELPHIA LIGHT HORSE TROOP FLAG is still in Philadelphia. A gold silk flag with 13 blue and silver stripes painted over the top of the King's Colors. Maybe that's an omen of something to come.

These fellows got Washington safely to Cambridge, and when they arrived, there were a thousand men waiting on their new commander and flying over their head was a flag no one had ever seen before.

It's in the history books.

It's called the GRAND UNION FLAG!

THE GRAND UNION FLAG

Don Hewitt

But, where did this idea come from?

Well, as I told you earlier, back in these days we thought we were English. Part of Mother England, and proud of it, but boy are we mad at the King.

And to show the King how mad we are, somebody had the nerve to take one of the King's flags, you remember?

The BRITISH RED ENSIGN.

Don Hewitt

Don Hewitt

Somebody took one of the king's flags and sewed six white strips of cloth on it to show that the colonies were united in the stripes, but separate from the Kings Colors in the corner.

And, we went to war under the GRAND UNION FLAG!

Well, we won a few battles and lost a few.
The first thing you know summer is coming on.
There's more people joining the Sons of Liberty.
We're calling for freedom and independence now.
And on the 4th of July 1776 we declared our independence!

Now we are a new nation, but boy we better win that war. Would you believe, that if we hadn't won all of our heroes could have been jailed, or executed, or worse than that, investigated by a special congressional committee. Ha! Ha!

Nobody wanted to fly that flag any more, so we fought on almost a year without a flag.

Then in 1777 Congress decided, "Here we are a new country putting ships to sea, trading, fighting a war. We're trying to get respect in the world. We've got to have identification."

On June 14th, 1777 Congress passed the first flag resolution, a simple paragraph. All it said was:

> "Resolved, the flag of the United States shall be thirteen alternate red and white stripes and thirteen white stars in a blue field representing a new constellation.*

"That's all they said.
No artwork.
No samples.
Just words.

* This resolution is paraphrased here. For the entire resolution see the front cover.

And in 1777 there were no flag factories.

All those flags were made by individual seamstresses.
Every village and hamlet,
every army unit,
every ship had their own seamstress.

And the words went out, describing the new flag of the United States.

There were no two alike.

Every seamstress made a different flag.

That's where I got the title,
"Many Faces of Old Glory,"

And here they come!

John B. Rodgers

One of the first examples took place in a little town we call Bennington, Vermont today. Back in these days it was still Bennington, New York. The Colonel of the Bennington Militia, Colonel John Stark, is about to go to war against the King, and his wife says, "John, if your going to fight for your country, you've got to have your country's flag."

So, she evidently had the description of the new flag. She's going to make her husband's flag. Well, the one she made is in the history books. It's called the BENNINGTON FLAG, named after her husband's Bennington Militia.

But, where did she get the idea to put white stripes on the outside? Or, for that matter, she's got seven points on the stars.

Well, the historians tell us back in these days the only official thing anybody could find in print about flag designs, were in the Rules of Heraldry in Europe and England, that said something like, "Alternating colors of stripes should begin and end with white." Stars had to have six or more points to even be a star.

THE BENNINGTON FLAG

Don Hewitt

Anything with five points, back in these days, wasn't called a star. Those were called rowels or spurs. And, Congress had said "Star". So, to her that meant six or more points. And as you can see, I guess she figured her husband was somewhere around a seven maybe.   Ha! Ha!

Well, he ran his wife's flag up the pole, gathered his men together, and in a direct quote from the history books Colonel Stark said, "Men, we're going against the King's army, and we're either going to win or my wife will be a widow!"

Boy, am I glad I wasn't in his outfit because all of a sudden the battle began.

And right away, he could see, he's not going to win the Battle of Bennington. The British general, General Burgoyne, is going to win. But, suddenly, over in the hills... Colonel Stark can hear cannons roaring, guns cracking, men shouting, "There's somebody coming to the rescue!"

But they're so far away he can't see them. So.....he tells the sergeant, "Get out the long glass!" The sergeant gets out the long glass. "Who's com'in to the rescue Sergeant?"

"Well, I'll tell you one thing Pilgrim, that ain't Spider Man. But they've got a flag like I've never seen before! " Ha! Ha!

Who was it coming to the rescue with a flag they've never seen? Could it have been....

THE CAPED CRUSADER? Ha! Ha! Ha!

John B. Rodgers

Now I had a boy in middle school just a couple of weeks ago yell out and say, "Now wait a minute. He wasn't even born yet." Ha! Ha! Ha!

Somebody shouted, "Hey, they've got a green flag with 13 rowels on it!"

Colonel Stark says, "That's Ethan Allen and the Green Mountain Boys. They're coming to the rescue!" And come they did.

Ethan Allen had captured Fort Ticonderoga from the British at Lake Champlain, dragged those cannon across the mountains and saved Colonel Stark at the Battle of Bennington flying their GREEN FLAG!

GREEN MOUNTAIN BOYS FLAG

Don Hewitt

Now, this isn't such a bad idea you know, these guys are fighting in the woods, they're crawling around in the weeds, they're hiding in the tall grass. Now you don't want to drag around a red and white striped flag doing that, right? Ha!

Five points. One of the first flags in our history books with five.
Nobody knows who made it.
One of these guys that didn't know anything about heraldry rules but, boy could they fight.
They'd already been through the battle of Bunker Hill. But, unfortunately, Ethan Allen was captured later by the British and spent the rest of the revolution in jail in England. When it was over they let him out. He came back home to the land of opportunity. One evening a lady asked me, "Was he the guy that started that furniture factory?*

But, what happened to Colonel Stark? His wife didn't become a widow that day or the next. In fact Colonel Stark became a general and out lived them all. He was the oldest surviving general of the Revolution, and Congress gave him a gift.
A section of land.

But it was in a place so awful, so terrible, they had to give it away. They called this awful place......Ohio. Ha! Ha!
We call his section of land Stark County now.
So....the next time your up in Canton Ohio where the Pro Football Hall of Fame is remember that's Stark County. And they remember Ethan Allen and they remembered his wife that made his flag. They named a hospital after her. She's in your history books, Molly Stark. Boy, if that isn't "Paul Harvey and the Rest of the Story!" Ha! Ha! Ha!

You know, history's exciting when you hear these guys.
*The Ethan Allen Furniture Factory

Well a little while ago we beat General Burgoyne at the battle of Bennington, but he got away from us. He ran right into the Battle of Saratoga and we beat him there, too. In fact we captured him.

When the French found out we had captured this great general, they said, "You know, maybe those crazy Americans can win their revolution. Let's give them some help." So, among other things, they gave us some ships. We put cannons on them, found volunteer sailors, put a man in charge, John Paul Jones.

He's getting these ships outfitted, ready for sea. He ordered the flag of the United States made from a seamstress. Meanwhile, he decided to name his ship the Bon Homme Richard, to honor an old friend of his, Benjamin Franklin, who was publishing Poor Richard's Almanac at the time.

Pretty soon he got those ships. Ran that flag up in the rigging and proudly set sail as the United States Navy under a flag known in history as the BON HOMME RICHARD FLAG.

But it only has twelve stars. I thought we had thirteen states.
 Well the historians tell us that communications were so bad because Al Gore* hadn't invented the Internet yet. Ha! Ha!
He couldn't find out whether Georgia had joined the Revolution. So, he went to sea under a twelve star flag.

I had a fellow in the audience just a couple weeks ago from Georgia. He wasn't too sure if they had joined yet. Ha! Ha!
*Vice President under President Bill Clinton

BON HOMME RICHARD FLAG

John B. Rodgers

Now he's at sea looking for a British fighting force, a squadron of warships, and he found them. Off the east coast of Scotland in the North Sea.

They began to move in on each other.
It's a place called Firth of Fourth.
They're getting closer and closer.
They're sizing each other up.
All of a sudden the British sailors fired a cannon shot,
hit the Bon Homme Richard right at the waterline.
Now she's really taking on water, but it started the battle.
That sea battle lasted for six hours.

John Paul Jones has got to do something. His ship is sinking right out from under him. He's looking over at the British warship. He's shot their mast away, they're stopped dead in the water and his sailors are so tired from the fight they're not going to last much longer.

 Your not going to believe what happened next."
Up walked Peter Arnet, from CNN. Ha! Ha!

Well, he's in all the wars, isn't he? Ha! Ha!

He said, "John Paul, what are you going to do?"
John Paul looked at him and uttered his famous words,
"I've not yet begun to fight!"
And with those words, he ordered every yard of canvas they could get into the rigging and they sailed that sinking ship, as fast as she'd go, right into the side of the British warship, swung aboard, tied up the crew and captured the ship.

But he had to cut the Bon Homme Richard loose, she's going down fast. And he watched his ship float away and sink to the bottom of the ocean and his colors went with it.

Now, here he is, on a captured British warship, with no flag.
They've got to get out of there.
They jury-rigged the mast back up, got enough canvas
in the air to sail into the nearby neutral Dutch port, Texel.

They dropped anchor.

They're frantically working on this shot-up British warship, trying to get her seaworthy again, when John Paul Jones ordered a boat lowered.
They rowed him into port. He probably looked up the Harbor Master, and he may have said something like this.
"Sir, my name is John Paul Jones, from the United States Navy.
We've captured this British warship in the harbor here.
We're gettin' her repaired, ready for sea. We're going home, but we can't sail. We lost our flag."

You see, back in these days you couldn't sail without a flag or they figured you were a pirate.

So, hc asked the Dutchman, "Does anyone here know what my country's new flag looks like?"

Would you believe that Dutchman had a drawing of the new flag of the United States?

**Where did
this drawing
come from?**

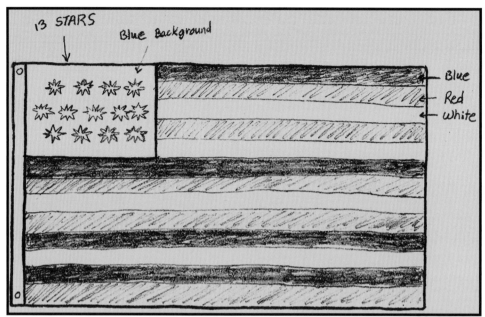

John B. Rodgers

Well, the historians tell us that earlier than this, our ambassador to France, who happened to be Benjamin Franklin, was in the French Parliament one day, and they asked Mr. Franklin. It may have gone something like this:

"Monsieur, you're a new country in the world, putting ships to sea, trading, fighting a war. Could you describe your country's new flag to the court artists here?

We make sketches, send them to the nearby ports, then we can recognize your ships at sea."

Ben thinks, "boy that's a good idea." So he's thinking back to the day they passed the first Flag Resolution.

Remember? I recited it to you earlier., describes the flag in detail.

So, he told the artists all about it. They made the drawings and sent them around. John Paul Jones got one of those drawings in the port of Texel, and had a Dutch seamstress make the flag.

He quickly went back to the captured ship. Ran it up in the riggings and proudly sailed for home under what he thought was the official flag of the United States, according to Benjamin Franklin.

But, there's a small problem. The historians think that Ben was asleep the day they passed the resolution.

Well, I always tell the kids, "This is what happens when you don't pay attention in class." Ha! Ha! Ha!

This is called the TEXEL FLAG named after the Dutch port where it was made.

The most amazing part of this story, John Paul Jones got home safe under this flag. I'm surprised the British, the Americans, the Huguenots, and everybody else weren't shooting at this.

THE TEXEL FLAG

John B. Rodgers

Now, he's a hero. So, the're building him a new flagship called the Alliance. It's almost finished when the ladies of Portsmouth, where they're building the ship, (*they don't want him to go to sea with this*) so they're going to make him the "Official Flag".

Well, the one they made is named after that ship.

This is called the
ALLIANCE FLAG.

THE ALLIANCE FLAG

John B. Rodgers

Well, here we have Heraldry rules again. White stripes on the outside, we're up to eight points on the stars now, you know the rule; six or more points.

One flag. One group of seamstresses, one ship.

There are no two flags alike.

John B. Rodgers

The Surrender of Cornwallis

Down south, one of the worst battles of the entire Revolution took place in a little town you could go through your whole life and never hear of it.

Unfortunately, we lost the battle, but while we were losing, we beat up Cornwallis' British Army so bad they never recovered.

And by the time they got to the Battle of Yorktown there wasn't enough fight left.

Cornwallis surrendered the British Army and the Revolution was over.

The beginning of the end of the British Army began with one of the worst battles of the Revolution in the little town of Guilford Court House North Carolina.

And those good-ol' boys fought for liberty under their stars and stripes, but they had a little problem about what it was supposed look like you see.

Well they heard that resolution with different ears than we did. The original GUILFORD COURTHOUSE FLAG hangs today in the museum in Raleigh-Durham North, Carolina, a relic of the worst flag of the entire- - -
Ha! Ha!

I mean, the worst battle of the entire Revolution.

GILFORD COURTHOUSE FLAG

Don Hewitt

Easton, Pennsylvania; We hid the Liberty Bell there on it's way to Allentown, so the British couldn't find it. They're going to fight the British and they've got to have a flag.

The ladies are saying, "Well, we'll make it."

But what are they going to make?

Remember the resolution; Thirteen alternate red and white stripes; thirteen white stars in a blue field.

What's so complicated about that?

Well, They didn't think it was. They knew exactly what Congress meant. You know, just like we do today. Ha! Ha!

They said according to Congress, this is the flag of the United States!

THE EASTON FLAG

John B. Rodgers

Well now, wait a minute. Thirteen alternate red and white stripes....there they are...they didn't say where. Thirteen white stars in a blue field. There they are, big as life.

Technically, you could almost say this flag is more correct than the one we fly today. The original EASTON FLAG is still there in the museum, and they still argue; was it in the rebellion or the War of 1812?

Well, about this time George Washington hears about all this. So he and a couple of Congressmen, (*We can't. You know, here we are trying to get respect in the world. We can't even make two flags that look alike*). So...he and a couple of Congressmen are going to get together and get the first official flag made right, because none of these are.

Well, here's where the historians reach the fork in the road.

Who made it? Well, a lot of them want to give the honor to a Congressman from New Jersey, Francis Hopkinson, because to this day they still have the bill he turned in for the design of the Great Seal of the United States and one flag. But, unfortunately, his flag didn't survive and there's no drawings or descriptions. Besides, there's no record of him ever being paid.

So that leaves the other historians.

Well, they want to give the great honor to a professional flag maker in Philadelphia.....Betsy Ross.

She was paid!

They've got her receipts for federal flags from the government, but unfortunately none of hers survived either, or any drawings. So, we can't prove for sure who made that first official flag, but the legend of Betsy Ross lives on.

Now, imagine the two Congressmen in her tiny living room talking about all these flags you've seen. Well, the men don't like the ones with Heraldry Rules, white stripes on the outside, because, on a bright sunshiny day those outside white stripes blend with the bright sky in the background. It looks like there's only eleven stripes. The flags look smaller. So, they decide to ignore the rules and put red stripes on the outside.

Well then, according to legend, Betsy Ross says, "Well, gentlemen, if your going to change the stripes. Can I do something with these stars?"

They said, "Well, what's the matter with the stars?"

She said, "Well, some of these ladies that are making flags are using six, seven, twelve....points. They're crooked, they're all different shapes and sizes, they're hard to make. With your permission, I'd like to use a five pointed star, because I can cut a perfect one with one cut of the scissors!"

Of course, that means she can make the flags faster. Anybody knows, when you work for the Federal Government you've got to be efficient. Ha! Ha!

Well, can you imagine how nervous Betsy Ross is, with the President of the United States in her living room?

You know, if you got up in the morning and found a strange guy in your living room, in tight, Robin-egg-Blue satin pantaloons, a cape, a white powdered wig, and buckles on his shoes and a linen shirt something like what I've got on ..... and a linen handkerchief!

"Is that Elton John I see?" Ha! Ha!

THE BETSY ROSS FLAG

Don Hewitt

She's going to make one cut.

And I hope I do this right.

One cut.

I don't hear anybody breathing.

Well, gee whiz look at that!

So, according to the legend of Betsy Ross, that's how we got the first official flag, but, there are a couple of mistakes you see. There's more than one version. This is the version that we grew up with. You know...thirteen stars in a circle.

We know and love the BETSY ROSS FLAG. But the historians tell us that most of those early flags, the thirteen stars were in straight, staggered lines just like they are today. But, this is an official flag and should be treated like one. The BETSY ROSS FLAG.

fold and cut 5 star

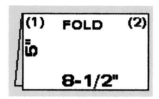

Step 1. Fold an 8-1/2" x 10" piece of paper in half.

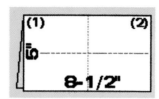

Step 2. Fold and unfold in half both ways to form creased center lines. (Note: be sure paper is still folded in half.)

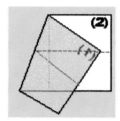

Step 3. Bring corner (1) right to meet the center line. Be sure to fold from the vertical crease line.

Step 4. Bring corner (1) left till edges coincide, then make the fold.

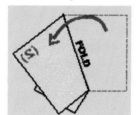

Step 5. Bring corner (2) left and fold.

Step 6. Bring corner (2) right until edges coincide. Then fold.

Step 7. Cut on the angle as shown in the picture. Then unfold the small piece.

Step 8. Marvel at your perfect (we hope!) 5-pointed star! If your star is not perfect, take a fresh piece of paper (8-1/2" x 10" — not 8-1/2" x 11") and return to Step 1.

ushistory.org home Copyright © 1995-2006 by the Independence Hall Association

Well, we won that war in case you missed history class that day. Now it's 1780, And John Hancock, the Governor of Massachusetts, awards the Massachusetts Black Company their flag. They were the free black slaves that fought valiantly in the revolution and gained the attention of the governor. Heroes in every sense of the word. Little attention has been given to them in our history books, including the American Indians that fought on the side of freedom.

MASSACHUSETTS BLACK COMPANY

John B. Rodgers

Well, the King says we didn't win anything!

He's stopping our ships at sea, kidnapping sailors. We're getting madder by the minute.

But, we took in two more states. Now we've got 15. The flag is wrong, already. So, we have to pass another resolution. Pretty much the same as the first, but they just changed the numbers to fifteen stars, fifteen stripes. Then we got into the war of 1812 with King George again and we fought it under that second official flag.

This is what it looked like when Francis Scott Key looked out the porthole, in the rocket's red glare, the bombs bursting in air and wrote our National

Anthem. That's why we call this, the STAR SPANGLED BANNER.

The reason he could see it at night, it was flying over Fort McHenry and was the largest battle flag ever flown....thirty by forty-two feet. The original flag is at the Smithsonian today, being totally restored so that your grandchildren and their grandchildren can go see this jewel of America.

THE STAR SPANGLED BANNER

Don Hewitt

Well, we won that war, but we took in five more states while we were fighting it. Now we're up to twenty.

What's Congress going to do? They gonna' keep doing the same thing.....

twenty stars, twenty stripes? You know, if they had kept that up, our fifty star flag today would have fifty stripes..............in a lapel pin? Well, they knew they were in trouble, so in 1818 they passed the third flag resolution:

> "Resolved, the flag of the United States shall be thirteen alternate red and white stripes to honor the original colonies, and one star for each state thereafter."

That's how we got back to thirteen stripes. The STAR SPANGLED BANNER is the only official flag that didn't have thirteen stripes.

What did that twenty star flag look like in 1818. Well, the historians tell us that a lot of them looked like this! The GREAT STAR FLAG obviously, but there were others. As we came down through the years and added more states and more stars to the blue field, there were other great star designs, but this was the first...the TWENTY STAR.

There's been twenty-seven official flags of the United States, beginning with Betsy Ross, right on up through these to the fifty star flag we fly today, which became official on the 4th of July 1960.

THE TWENTY STAR FLAG

John B. Rodgers

The stories you have heard tonight have invested our nation's flag with much historical meaning. But it's up to each person of every generation to understand and appropriate the meaning of the flag for themselves. President Woodrow Wilson once said, "This flag which we honor and under which we serve is the emblem of our unity, our power, our thought and purpose, as a nation. It has no other character than that which we give it. From generation to generation the choices are ours."

When our great banner of freedom was first raised hopes and dreams were high for a perfect union. Our forefathers had fought and died for the principals of the Bill of Rights. They believed those benefits would come to all future generations of Americans.

The flag they raised that day was pure and proud with no past, only a future to be built on those same foundations. The soft breezes of life, liberty and the pursuit of happiness that caressed their flag that April's day still exist but unfortunately not for all Americans. Along with all the benefits that we enjoy as Americans, there are also obligations. You may be born an American, which is one thing, but being an American is quite another. We must continue to build on those same foundations, not only as a nation but as individuals, working together to create that perfect union with Liberty & Justice for all.

And so, to all the young men and women who have ever served or are serving the cause of freedom around the world. If you've ever had any doubts about why?

I give you this:

Our National Athem

Oh! say, can you see, by the dawn's early light,
What so proudly we hailed at the twilight's last gleaming?
Whose broad stripes and bright stars, thro' the perilous fight,
O'er the ramparts we watched, were so gallantly streaming?
And the rockets' red glare, the bombs bursting in air,
Gave proof thro' the night that our flag was still there.
Oh! say, does that Star-Spangled Banner yet wave
O'er the land of the free and the home of the brave?

The Don Hewitt paintings seen in this book appear in an unique Historical Flag collection which is on display as a part of a continuing patriotic educational program conducted by Greater Pittsburgh Council, Boy Scouts of America, in its Scout Center located at Flag Plaza near Civic Arena in the uptown area, Pittsburgh, Pennsylvania.

A colorful flag ceremony honoring many of the flags depicted in this booklet is conducted by request at Flag Plaza and may be viewed by the public. Further information may be obtained from Greater Pittsburgh Council, Boy Scouts of America, Flag Plaza, Pittsburgh, Pennsylvania 15219, Telephone area code (412) 471-2927.

Flag Plaza is a gift in trust to Greater Pittsburgh Council, Boy Scouts of America, for this and succeeding generations of young Americans. It is given in memory of Chester Hamilton Lehman, a distinguished citizen, industrialist, and Scouter of Southwestern Pennsylvania, by Vivian W. Lehman.

TO ORDER DVD/VHS CASSETTE

VANE SCOTT DVD/VIDEO
BOX 1776, Newcomerstown, OH 43832
Send check or money order for $29.95 each for VHS and
$34.95 for DVD plus $3.50 for shipping and handling.
Schools and Libraries write for special packages and rates.
(740) 498-8803   >www.vanescott.com<